I Like Holidays!

# WHAT IS VETERANS DAY?

**Elaine Landau**

**Enslow Elementary**

an imprint of

**Enslow Publishers, Inc.**

40 Industrial Road
Box 398
Berkeley Heights, NJ 07922
USA

http://www.enslow.com

# CONTENTS

# WORDS TO KNOW

**Armed Forces**—The five parts of America's military. They protect America's freedom. These are the Army, Navy, Marines, Air Force, and Coast Guard.

**holiday**—A day of celebration.

**military [MIHL ih tair ee]**—Having to do with the Armed Forces or fighting in a war. The military protects people from attacks from other countries. They help with natural disasters, such as floods. They help keep peace around the world.

**patriotic [pay tree AH tik]**—Showing love for your country.

**veteran [VEH tur ihn]**—A person who has served in the Armed Forces.

# A SPECIAL DAY

What special day is this? There are parades.
People bring flowers to soldiers' graves.
We thank those who have served in the
Armed Forces. It must be Veterans Day.

# OUR VETERANS

Veterans are people who have served in the Armed Forces. They have kept our country safe and free. They have put their lives in danger to do this. Many have died for our freedom.

These veterans are at a ceremony at Arlington National Cemetery, Virginia, on Veterans Day, 2010.

This soldier visits a kindergarten class on Veterans Day. They play a marching game.

# BECAUSE WE ARE
# FREE

We can go to school because we are free and safe. We can live where we want because we are free and safe. We can say what we think because we are free and safe.

# IT'S A
# HOLIDAY

Veterans Day is on November 11. It is a day to honor our veterans. November 11 was the day World War 1 ended in 1918. The day became a holiday in 1954.

# SPEECHES

On Veterans Day, there are many special events. We hear speeches thanking these brave men and women. The veterans speak, too. They tell us about their time in the service.

President Obama gives a speech on Veterans Day.

# PARADES

Many towns have parades. Some parades are very big. Veterans march. Military bands play. People come out to cheer. They clap for the heroes and wave small flags.

# REMEMBERING
# HEROES

People visit veterans' graves on this day. They bring flowers. Some people fly our country's flag in front of their home. They want veterans to know that we care. They want to thank the veterans for keeping us free and safe.

# WE
# HONOR
# THEM

Veterans have done so much for
our nation. They have kept us
safe and free over the years.
We can never thank them enough.
So we honor them on Veterans Day.

President Obama honors some war veterans.

# WHAT YOU CAN DO: AN ACTIVITY

## You Will Need:

- ❖ Poster board
- ❖ Magic markers (different colors)
- ❖ Paste
- ❖ Pictures of men and women in the Armed Forces. You can find lots of these on the Internet or in magazines. Be creative! Pick pictures of men and women serving in different wars. Find pictures of the American flag and some military medals too.

## Make a Veterans Day thank you poster!

Is there a veteran in your family? Do you know a veteran in your neighborhood? This Veterans Day, be patriotic! Let that person know how you feel. Make a Veterans Day Thank You Poster.

20

# What to Do:

❖ In the center of the poster, write some words, such as "Thank You for Your Service."

❖ Paste the different pictures around the words.

❖ Sign your name at the bottom. Ask your family, friends, and neighbors to sign too.

❖ Give the poster to a veteran on Veterans Day. Expect to see a big smile on that person's face!

# LEARN MORE

## BOOKS

Reed, Jennifer. *The U.S. Navy*. Mankato, Minn.: Capstone Press, 2009.

Schaefer, Ted, and Lola M. *The Vietnam Veterans Memorial*. Chicago: Heinemann's Library, 2006.

Simmons, Lisa Bolt. *Soldiers of the U.S. Army*. Mankato, Minn.: Capstone Press, 2009.

Walker, Robert. *Veteran's Day*. New York: Crabtree, 2010.

# WEB SITES

VA Kids.
   http://www.va.gov/kids/k-5/index.asp

Veterans Day Wreath
   http://www.first-school.ws/t/cp_seasonal/us_veteran.html

# INDEX

Enslow Elementary, an imprint of Enslow Publishers, Inc.

Enslow Elementary® is a registered trademark of Enslow Publishers, Inc.

Copyright © 2012 by Elaine Landau

**Library of Congress Cataloging-in-Publication Data**

Landau, Elaine.
  What is Veterans Day? / by Elaine Landau.
    p. cm. — (I like holidays!)
  Includes index.
  Summary: "An introduction to Veterans Day with an easy activity"—Provided by publisher.
  ISBN 978-0-7660-3705-2
  1. Veterans Day—Juvenile literature.  I. Title.
  D671.L37 2012
  394.264—dc22
                    2010039479

Paperback ISBN 978-1-59845-290-7

Printed in China

052011 Leo Paper Group, Heshan City, Guangdong, China

10 9 8 7 6 5 4 3 2 1

**Photo Credits:** Department of Defense (DOD): photo by Cherie Cullen, pp. 1, 7, photo by Jay Field, pp. 3 (holiday), 14, photo by John B. Snyder, p. 11, photo by Rachel Poonder, APG News, p. 8, photo by Sgt. Opal Vaughn, pp. 13, 19, photo by Tech Sgt Brian E. Christiansen, p. 4, photo by Tom Budzyna, p. 16, photo by Tonya K. Townsell, p. 21; Shutterstock.com, pp. 2, 3 (armed forces, patriotic, veteran), 15, 23.

**Cover Photo:** ©iStockphoto.com/PinkTag

Series Consultant:
Duncan R. Jamieson, PhD
Professor of History
Ashland University
Ashland, OH

Series Literacy Consultant:
Allan A. De Fina, PhD
Dean, College of Education
Professor of Literacy Education
New Jersey City University
Past President of the New Jersey
Reading Association